PICTURE-PERFECT SAT VOCAB

The Visual Learner's Vocabulary Guide

Sunny Williams

Dedicated to Beryl Moore a lifelong lover of language

INTRODUCTION

At are core, we are all visual learners. That what makes this learning approach so powerful. Words shape the way we think, read, write, and communicate. A strong vocabulary is a foundation for academic success and deeper understanding. Whether you are preparing for the SAT, strengthening your reading comprehension, or simply expanding your command of English, the words in this book are designed to help you build lasting verbal skills that extend beyond a single exam.

The SAT rewards students who can recognize *nuance*, interpret tone, understand complex passages, and distinguish between closely related ideas. Many of the words in this book appear frequently in advanced reading, literature, academic writing, journalism, and college-level coursework. By mastering them, you are developing the language skills needed for higher education and professional communication.

This book approaches vocabulary learning visually and contextually. Each word is paired with carefully designed illustrations, definitions, symbolic imagery, and example sentences intended to reinforce meaning through association and memory. Instead of memorizing isolated definitions, you will encounter words as ideas connected to situations, emotions, contrasts, and patterns. This helps transform passive recognition into active understanding and builds a more *coherent* grasp of language.

As you work through the pages, pay close attention to recurring relationships between words. Some terms describe precision and clarity, such as *lucid*, *meticulous*, and *discerning*. Others explore uncertainty and ambiguity, including *equivocal* and *vague.* You will also encounter words tied to human behavior, reasoning, conflict, integrity, emotion, and persuasion. Recognizing these conceptual families can dramatically improve retention and reading comprehension while helping you avoid a *myopic* approach to learning vocabulary one word at a time.

The most effective way to study vocabulary is through repeated exposure and active usage. Be *diligent* in revisiting difficult words and *persistent* in applying them in your own writing and conversation. Pause to predict meanings before reading definitions, and try to notice subtle differences between related terms. The goal is not short-term memorization, but long-term fluency and an *intuitive* understanding of language.

At the end of the book, you will find a set of review and test questions designed to help reinforce comprehension and measure progress. These exercises encourage you to apply the vocabulary in context, distinguish between related meanings, and strengthen recall under test-like conditions. Use them not only to assess yourself, but also to identify which words require additional review. Even students who feel *ambivalent* about standardized testing often discover that vocabulary study improves their overall confidence in reading and writing.

Vocabulary growth is cumulative. Over time, concepts that once seemed *obscure* become clear, and difficult passages become more *accessible* and *lucid.* With consistent practice, the words in this book will become part of your working vocabulary—tools you can use with precision.

Good luck, study consistently, and approach each new word with curiosity. The ability to communicate with clarity, insight, and *integrity* is one of the most valuable academic skills you can develop.

ILLUSTRATED VOCABULARY

VOLATILE

unstable and likely to change suddenly

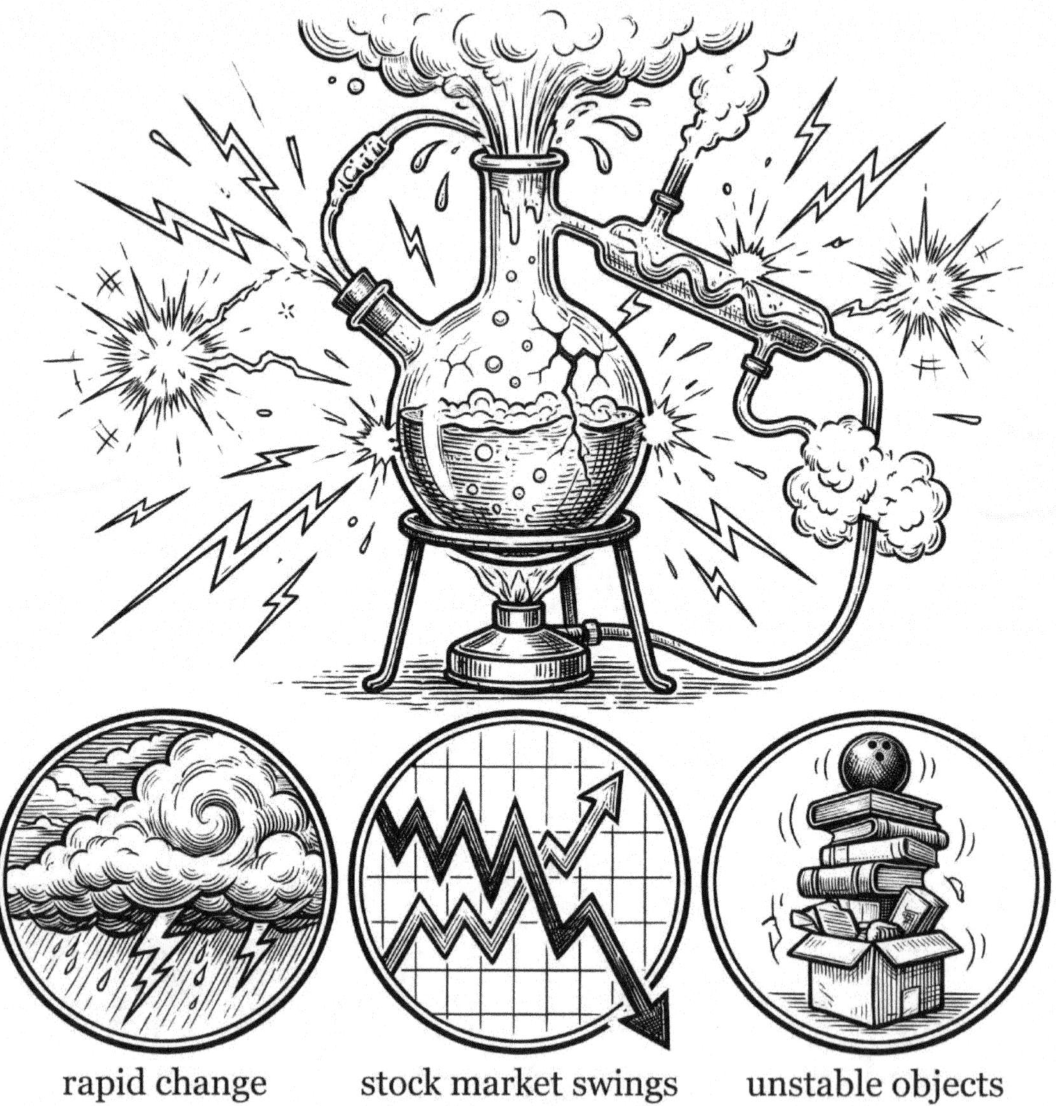

rapid change | stock market swings | unstable objects

examples

- The chemical reaction was highly **volatile**, requiring immediate evacuation.
- His temper was extremely **volatile**, shifting from calm to rage without warning.
- The **volatile** nature of the political landscape made predictions impossible.

CONSTRAINT

a limitation or restriction

narrow doorway restricting movement

budget ledger limiting choices

rapidly ticking clock reducing available time

- The construction project faced a significant constraint due to a shortage of skilled labor.
- Strict environmental regulations act as a constraint on industrial development in the area.
- Limited storage space is a major constraint for the growing business.

CONFLICTING

in disagreement or opposition; incompatible

opposing forces **incompatible elements** **divergent viewpoints**

examples

- The retired athlete's desire for excitement conflicts with his need for rest.
- The proposed solution is conflicting with our core values.
- The new policy has conflicting goals that are hard to reconcile.

OBSCURE

unclear, hidden, or difficult to understand

faded manuscript

distant object in heavy fog

hidden pathways

examples

- the ancient text's meaning remained obscure due to the faded script and missing pages.
- dense fog made the distant coastline obscure, rendering navigation difficult and dangerous.
- her motives for the sudden departure were obscure, leaving everyone puzzled and uncertain.

AUTHENTIC

genuine; real; not false or copied.

verified seal truthful reflection genuine vs. fake

examples

- The museum verified the painting as an AUTHENTIC Rembrandt after extensive analysis.
- He appreciated her AUTHENTIC personality, as she never tried to be someone else.
- Only AUTHENTIC parts should be used for the vintage car restoration to maintain its value.

MYOPIC

lacking foresight or broad perspective; narrow-minded

keyhole view vs. open door *telescope on nearby objects* *cutting fruit tree for firewood*

examples

- His myopic approach to the budget focused only on immediate savings, completely overlooking the long-term costs of neglect.
- The company's myopic strategy of pursuing short-term profits led to its eventual downfall as competitors invested in future technologies.
- She demonstrated a myopic view of the problem, considering only its current symptoms rather than addressing the root causes for a lasting solution.

FRAGMENTED

broken into disconnected parts.

disconnected train tracks | torn pages of a book | broken communication signals

examples

- The ancient vase was found in FRAGMENTED pieces, requiring careful restoration.
- His memory of the accident was FRAGMENTED, with only flashes of clarity.
- The organization became FRAGMENTED after the merger, with teams working in isolation.

CASTIGATE

to reprimand someone severely.

a stinging whip cracking violently.

a heavy ruler striking a desk.

an accusing finger pointing sharply.

examples

- The coach **castigated** the team for their lack of effort during the crucial game.
- After the scandalous report, the CEO was **castigated** by the board of directors.
- She knew her parents would **castigate** her severely for breaking the heirloom vase.

TRUCULENT

eager or quick to argue or fight; aggressively defiant.

growling bulldog straining against a spiked collar.

two rams clashing horns violently on a narrow mountain pass.

clenched fist covered in heavy leather wraps.

examples

- The **truculent** customer refused to pay the bill, shouting threats and knocking over a display.
- His **truculent** attitude made him unpopular with his colleagues, who often avoided him.
- The **truculent** mob charged the police line, throwing rocks and shouting insults.

EBULLIENT

cheerful and full of energy.

pot of water bubbling completely over the brim.

champagne bottle popping with a massive burst of fizz.

cluster of balloons soaring freely into the open sky.

examples

- Her **ebullient** personality always brightened up the room.
- The **ebullient** crowd cheered loudly as their team scored the winning goal.
- He felt **ebullient** after receiving the incredible news about his promotion.

PERFIDIOUS

deceitful and untrustworthy.

handshake with hidden dagger.

snake in a beautiful bouquet.

torn treaty with spilled ink.

examples

- The general was **perfidious**, leading his troops into a trap set by the enemy.
- His **perfidious** nature was revealed when he betrayed his closest friend for personal gain.
- The **perfidious** act of leaking confidential information completely destroyed their alliance.

PHLEGMATIC

having an unemotional and stolidly calm disposition.

still pool
reflecting storm.

stone statue amidst
overgrown vines.

tortoise steadily
passing racing hares.

examples

- The **phlegmatic** general remained calm during the chaos of battle, making clear decisions.
- Despite the alarming news, his response was **phlegmatic** and lacked any sense of urgency.
- She maintained a **phlegmatic** demeanor throughout the intense negotiation, never revealing her strategy.

DISTORT

to twist or misrepresent something.

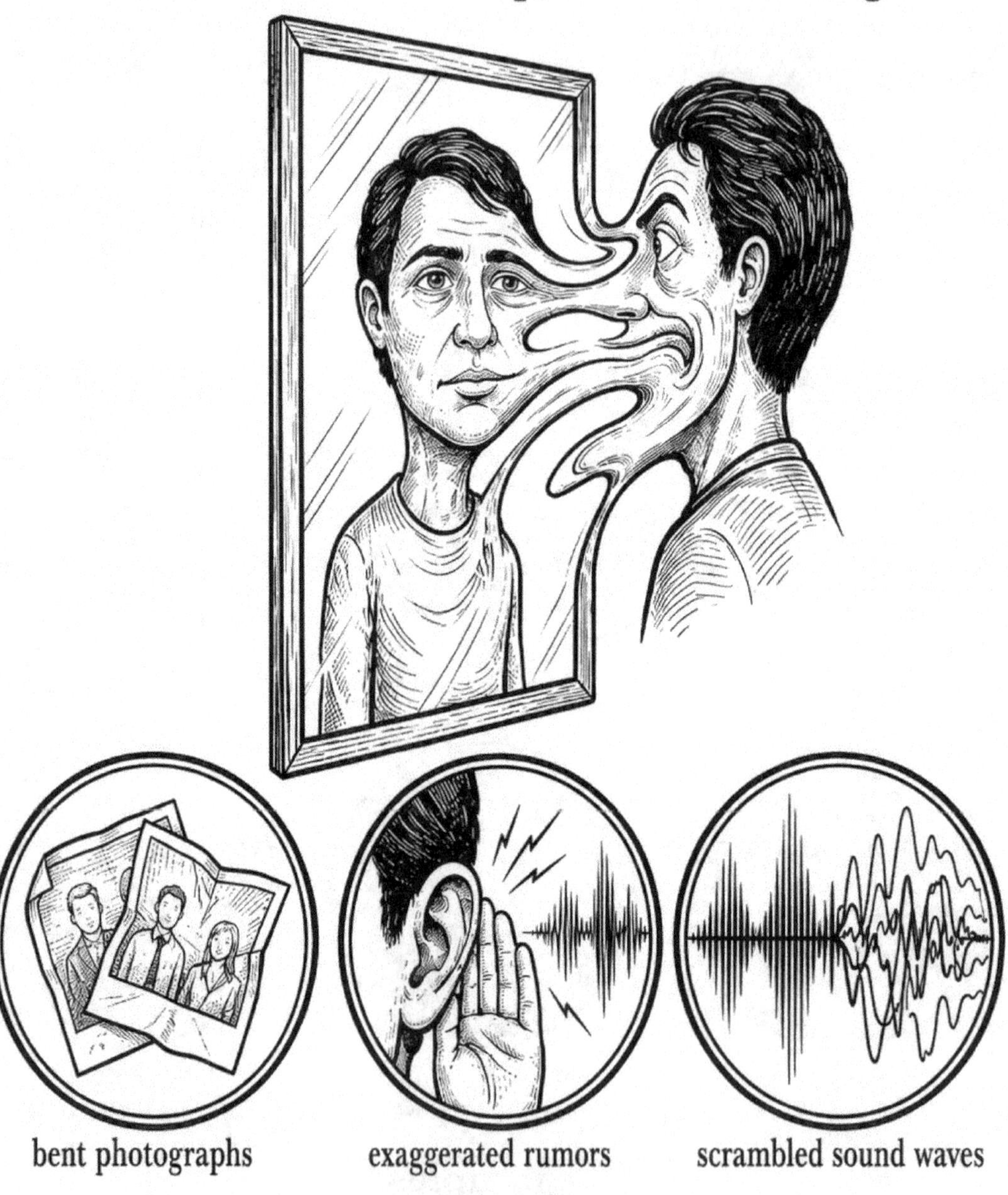

bent photographs exaggerated rumors scrambled sound waves

examples

- The media tends to **DISTORT** the facts to fit their narrative.
- The broken glass **DISTORTED** the reflection of the street outside.
- His anger made him **DISTORT** the truth about what happened.

INTRANSIGENT

unwilling or refusing to change one's views or to agree about something

massive boulder blocking a fast-flowing river.

heavily rusted padlock that cannot be opened.

old oak tree standing completely rigid in hurricane-force winds.

examples

- The negotiator remained **intransigent**, refusing to make any concessions despite the urgency.
- Her **intransigent** stance on the issue prevented any chance of a compromise.
- Despite clear evidence, the committee was **intransigent** and denied the proposal.

DECISIVE

able to make decisions quickly and confidently

chess player making bold move

judge striking gavel.

traveler cutting ropes

examples

- The general was decisive, ordering an immediate advance that secured victory.
- Her decisive action in the emergency saved valuable time and resources.
- A decisive leader is essential for navigating complex organizational challenges.

DILIGENT

showing steady and careful effort in work or duties.

tending rows over time. repeated revisions. steady shaping.

examples

- She was **diligent** in her studies, earning top grades in every subject.
- The team's **diligent** preparation led to a flawless presentation.
- Through **diligent** practice, the musician mastered the complex piece.

CHICANERY

the use of trickery to achieve a political, financial, or legal purpose.

a shell game being rigged

a contract with misleading fine print

a fox wearing a sheep's fleece

examples

- The investigation revealed that the company engaged in **chicanery** to win the lucrative government contract.
- Political opponents accused the senator of using **chicanery** to manipulate the voting results.
- The lawyer's **chicanery** during the trial confused the jury and ultimately led to a mistrial.

NUANCE

a subtle difference or distinction.

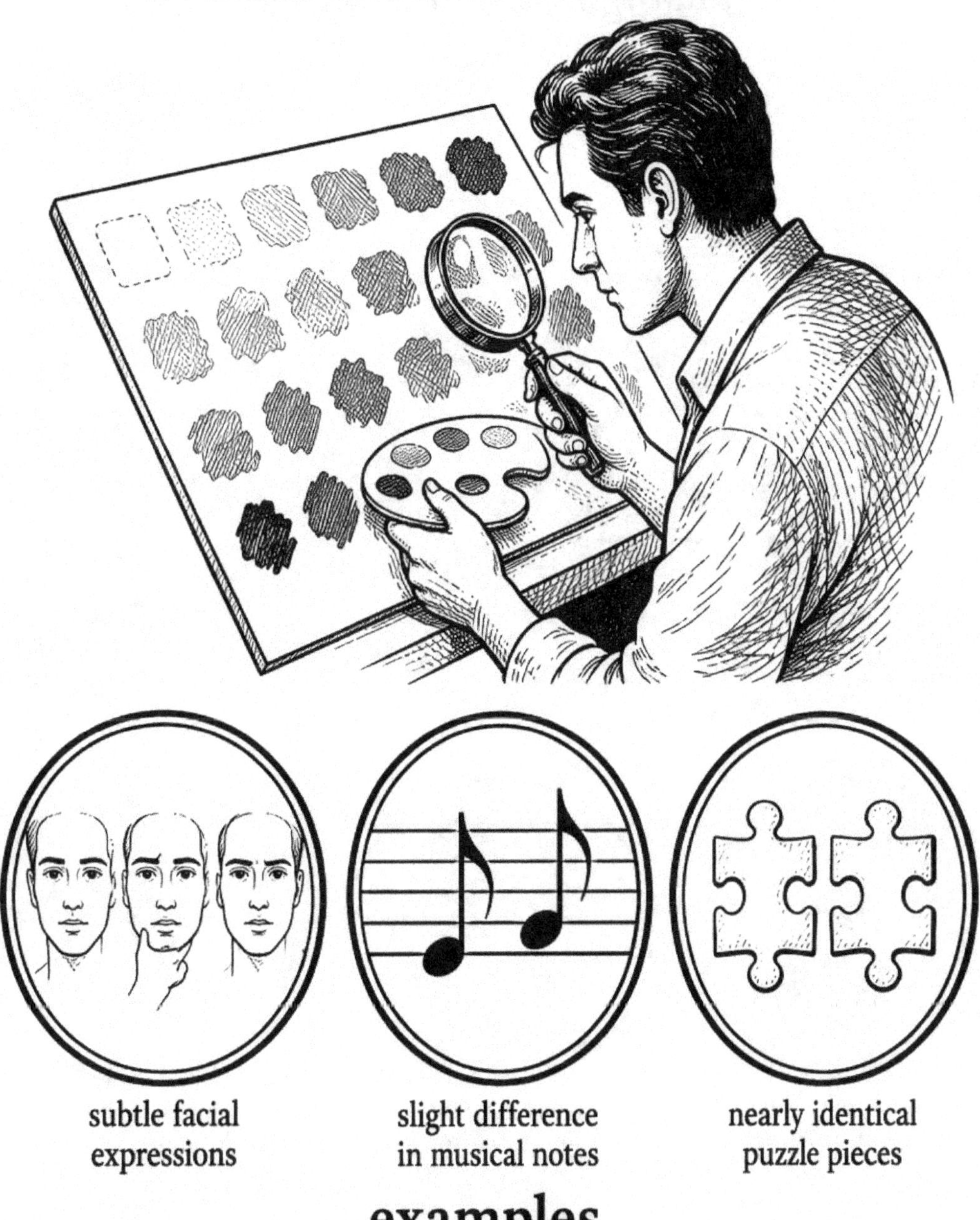

subtle facial expressions

slight difference in musical notes

nearly identical puzzle pieces

examples

- The actor's performance relied on nuance to make a complex character visibly human.
- Understanding the nuance between the two languages makes translation a fine art.
- She appreciated the difference in the wine's nuance of berry and spice.

DELETERIOUS

causing harm or damage

a moth steadily eating through fine fabric

aggressive rust consuming an iron gear

a drop of acid burning a hole through a delicate leaf

examples

- The company's new policy had a **deleterious** effect on employee morale.
- Prolonged exposure to the sun can have **deleterious** consequences for skin health.
- The **deleterious impact** of the chemical spill was felt for years.

ERUDITE

having deep and extensive knowledge

annotated manuscripts | interconnected disciplines | attentive students

examples

- The professor's *erudite* lectures on ancient civilizations were both informative and engaging.
- She was known for her *erudite* understanding of quantum mechanics and its philosophical implications.
- The book provides an *erudite* analysis of the economic and social factors leading to the revolution.

AMBIVALENT

having mixed or contradictory feelings about something.

uneven balance of feelings.

coexisting contradictory emotions.

hesitation at diverging paths.

examples

- She felt *ambivalent* about the job offer, appreciative of the salary but worried about the long hours.
- His feelings toward his hometown were *ambivalent*, loving the memories but hating the lack of opportunity.
- The committee was *ambivalent* about the new policy, recognizing its benefits but fearing its potential drawbacks.

PARADOX

a seemingly contradictory statement that may contain truth.

examples

- "The only constant in life is change" is a classic paradox.
- He is a wise fool, often speaking profound truths in simple jests.
- Deep down, you're really shallow.

PRISTINE

in perfect original condition; pure and unspoiled.

unmarked snow — preserved manuscript — flawless glass

examples

- The explorers were amazed by the PRISTINE wilderness, unseen by human eyes before.
- The museum curator handled the PRISTINE artifact with extreme care to maintain its condition.
- Despite the years, the vintage car was in PRISTINE condition, looking brand new.

UBIQUITOUS

present, appearing, or found everywhere.

ants swarming over every inch of a dropped picnic.

dandelions sprouting through every single crack in a brick sidewalk.

overlapping signal waves blanketing an entire globe.

examples

- The new smartphone app quickly became **ubiquitous** among teenagers.
- Plastic bags are unfortunately **ubiquitous** in our environment.
- Her influence was **ubiquitous** throughout the company's departments.

SUBJECTIVE

based on personal opinions, feelings, or perspectives.

varied opinions | emotional reactions to a movie | opinions about performance

examples

- Art appreciation is highly SUBJECTIVE, and people see beauty in different things.
- The quality of a movie is SUBJECTIVE and depends on each person's taste.
- Whether a performance was good or bad is SUBJECTIVE and varies by fan.

SUPERCEDE

to take the place of; to surpass or excel.

replacing the old surpassing others outdated by progress

examples

- The new leader's vision and innovation allowed her to supercede her predecessor's outdated policies.
- In just a few years, she worked tirelessly and superceded all others in her field.
- As technology advances, older methods are quickly superceded by more efficient solutions.

ALACRITY

brisk and cheerful readiness.

dog immediately leaping to fetch a thrown ball.

student enthusiastically raising their hand in a classroom.

ship's crew quickly hoisting sails at dawn.

examples

- The volunteers responded with **alacrity** to the call for help after the storm.
- She accepted the new project with **alacrity**, eager to prove her skills.
- The team moved with **alacrity** to complete the tasks before the deadline.

INDIGENT

poor or lacking basic necessities.

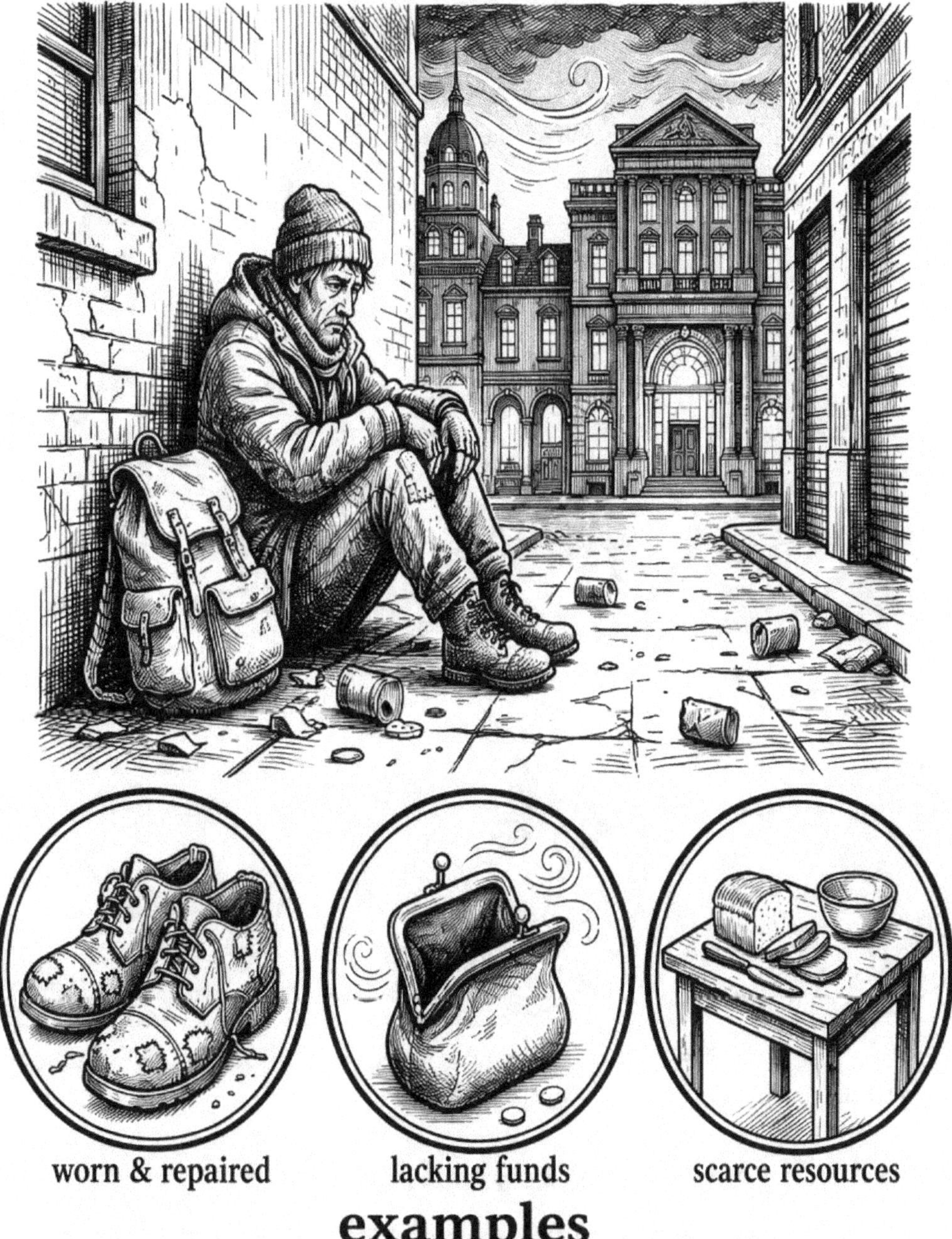

worn & repaired | lacking funds | scarce resources

examples

- The **INDIGENT** family could only afford a single meal each day.
- Many **INDIGENT** individuals seek shelter in community centers during harsh weather.
- Despite his **INDIGENT** circumstances, he never lost his dignity or hope.

PRAGMATIC

dealing with things realistically and practically.

sturdy boots over decorative shoes for difficult travel.

selecting durable materials over ornate decorations.

adjusting sails realistically to changing winds.

examples

- the pragmatic leader focused on immediate solutions rather than abstract theories.
- a pragmatic approach to city planning prioritizes functional infrastructure over cosmetic upgrades.
- faced with a budget shortfall, the committee made a pragmatic decision to cut non-essential programs.

ANACHRONISM

something placed outside its proper historical time period.

a knight using a laptop.

a steam locomotive passing futuristic skyscrapers.

a digital clock in an ancient temple.

examples

- The presence of a wristwatch in the historical drama was a glaring anachronism.
- His use of modern slang in the Civil War documentary was considered a major anachronism.
- The painting features an anachronism: a telephone on a desk from the 18th century.

ENERVATE

to cause someone to feel drained of energy or vitality; weaken.

battery losing its final spark of charge

wilted plant drooping over a dry pot

heavy iron anchor dragging down a tired swimmer

examples

- The prolonged heatwave began to **enervate** even the most energetic citizens.
- A lack of challenging work can **enervate** an otherwise ambitious employee.
- The constant, tedious meetings served only to **enervate** the entire team.

OPAQUE

difficult to understand; not transparent

unreadable documents fogged glass tangled chains

examples

- The company's financial reports were notoriously *opaque*, making it difficult for investors to assess its true value.
- Her motivations remained *opaque* to everyone, leading to much speculation and confusion.
- The dense, *opaque* fog blanketed the valley, obscuring all visibility and delaying travel.

OBFUSCATE

to deliberately make something unclear or difficult to understand.

maze hiding path | tangled text | fog and signs

examples

- The politician used legal jargon to *obfuscate* the truth about the new law.
- She tried to *obfuscate* the issue with irrelevant facts and figures.
- His explanation was so complex it only served to *obfuscate* the situation.

MISANTHROPE

a person who dislikes or distrusts humanity.

withdraws from social gatherings

erects barriers against others

abandons social facades

examples

- After years of betrayal, he became a misanthrope, living alone in a cabin and avoiding all human contact.
- The author's latest novel was criticized for its misanthropic tone, portraying every character as deeply flawed and selfish.
- Her misanthropy was evident in her cynical remarks about charitable acts and her refusal to trust anyone's intentions.

LUGUBRIOUS

looking or sounding sad and dismal.

wilted black rose.

lone hound howling silhouetted.

cracked gravestone covered in moss.

examples

- The **lugubrious** melody of the funeral dirge echoed through the empty church, filling it with sorrow.
- With a **lugubrious** expression, he recounted the series of misfortunes that had befallen his family.
- The dark, rain-soaked streets and gray skies created a **lugubrious** atmosphere that matched his mournful mood.

INSULAR

isolated; narrow-minded; from lack of contact with others.

closed off to outside ideas | limited perspective | narrow view

examples

- His INSULAR attitude made it difficult for him to collaborate with colleagues who had different backgrounds.
- The INSULAR culture in the village limited the young people's opportunities to pursue their dreams.
- Because of an INSULAR education, he was surprised by how diverse and dynamic the world truly is.

examples

- His directions were very **VAGUE**, leading us to get lost.
- The plan for the project was **VAGUE** and lacked specific goals.
- She gave a **VAGUE** answer, avoiding any direct details.

CONVENTIONAL

following traditional or widely accepted ways.

standard uniforms | traditional classroom seating | recipe followed exactly

examples

- The architect's design was highly conventional, featuring standard materials and layouts. She chose a conventional career path, studying law and joining a large firm.
- The wedding followed a conventional format, with traditional vows and reception.

LAMENT

to mourn or express deep sorrow.

deep mourning | sorrowful expression | mourning loss

examples

- The restless poet began to LAMENT the passing of her beloved mentor.
- She could not help but LAMENT the loss of her father, who had guided her through life's most difficult times.
- His mournful song was a public LAMENT for the injustices of the past.

ALTRUISTIC

showing selfless concern for the well-being of others.

sharing resources | lending a hand | passing the torch

examples

- The ALTRUISTIC nurse volunteered her time and expertise to help the disaster victims without any expectation of reward.
- His ALTRUISTIC donation to the children's hospital ensured that many families received the support they desperately needed.
- Despite her own challenges, her ALTRUISTIC nature led her to organize a community food drive every holiday season.

MITIGATE

to reduce the severity of something.

medicine easing pain | umbrella reducing rain effects | firefighters containing flames

examples

- The new seawalls helped to MITIGATE the impact of the storm surge.
- Doctors prescribed medication to MITIGATE the patient's discomfort.
- Prompt action by the firefighters helped to MITIGATE the spread of the blaze.

ASCERTAIN

to discover or determine with certainty.

confirming suspicions | obtaining information | arriving at facts

examples

- The detective used evidence to **ASCERTAIN** the true identity of the culprit.
- After years of research, the scientist was able to **ASCERTAIN** the properties of the new element.
- It is important to **ASCERTAIN** all the facts before making a decision.

CLANDESTINE

kept secret or done secretly

hidden messages | vanishing footprints | concealed meetings

examples

- The spies held a **clandestine** meeting in the abandoned warehouse to exchange classified information.
- Their **clandestine** relationship was kept secret from their families for many years.
- The government conducted a **clandestine** operation to infiltrate the enemy organization.

AFFLUENT

wealthy; having an abundance of money or resources.

overflowing wealth | luxurious dining | richly furnished

examples

- The AFFLUENT businessman donated millions to build a new hospital wing for the city.
- She came from an AFFLUENT family and was accustomed to a life of luxury and privilege.
- The neighborhood was known for its AFFLUENT residents, sprawling mansions, and private security.

MALLEABLE

easily shaped, influenced, or changed.

flexible metal wire | absorbing knowledge | soft wax wax

examples

- The artist used MALLEABLE clay to sculpt intricate figures, reshaping them until they were perfect.
- His opinions were surprisingly MALLEABLE; a persuasive argument could easily change his perspective on the issue.
- The young student's mind was MALLEABLE, quickly absorbing and adapting to new concepts taught in class.

METICULOUS

showing great attention to detail; very careful and precise

organized records

flawless hedges

exact proportions

examples

- The detective's *meticulous* investigation uncovered every hidden clue.
- She was known for her *meticulous* planning of every event down to the last detail.
- His *meticulous* restoration of the antique painting brought it back to its original glory.

LETHARGIC

sluggish; lacking energy or enthusiasm.

drooping plant deprived of sunlight.

dim lantern nearly extinguished.

person slowly dragging heavy chains.

examples

- After the long illness, he felt too LETHARGIC to get out of bed for days.
- The heat made the afternoon feel LETHARGIC, and no one wanted to work.
- Despite the approaching deadline, the team's progress remained LETHARGIC.

examples

- Despite the festive atmosphere, he remained PENSIVE, lost in memories of the past.
- Her journal was filled with PENSIVE entries, detailing her innermost thoughts and reflections.
- The old man sat by the window in a PENSIVE mood, watching the rain fall.

OSTENTATIOUS

designed to attract notice through excessive display

overly decorated mansion | excessive fireworks | displaying luxury items

examples

- The billionaire's **OSTENTATIOUS** yacht became a symbol of his extreme wealth.
- Her **OSTENTATIOUS** jewelry drew stares from everyone at the charity gala.
- The film premiere was an **OSTENTATIOUS** display of glamour and excess.

CACOPHONY

a harsh mixture of loud and unpleasant sounds.

clashing instruments

shrieking birds

tangled sound waves

examples

- The street market was a *cacophony* of shouting voices, honking horns, and blaring music.
- The band's experimental piece concluded in a *cacophony* of dissonant chords and clashing cymbals.
- The sudden *cacophony* of construction work outside my window made it impossible to concentrate.

TENACIOUS

persistent and determined; unwilling to give up.

breaks up obstacles | won't be uprooted | persistent efforts

examples

- Despite the weather reports, the TENACIOUS team kept ascending the mountain to summit.
- Her pursuit of TENACIOUS dedication to her research finally led to a breakthrough discovery.
- He didn't give up; his TENACIOUS spirit kept him going hour after hour until he finished.

ALIENATION

a feeling of isolation or separation from others.

disconnected line | separated from group | drifting alone

examples

- The new student felt a profound sense of alienation in the unfamiliar school.
- His unorthodox views led to his alienation from his former political party.
- Prolonged social media use can sometimes foster feelings of alienation despite digital connections.

VACILLATE

to waver between choices or opinions.

flickering compass alternating emotions moving balance scale

examples

- The politician continued to VACILLATE between the two proposals, unable to make a firm decision.
- She began to VACILLATE when presented with the conflicting evidence, unsure of which path to take.
- His tendency to VACILLATE on important matters often led to missed opportunities and confusion.

FASTIDIOUS

extremely attentive to detail; difficult to please.

jeweler's precision | symmetrical arrangement | correcting tiny flaw

examples

- The *fastidious* editor insisted on correcting every single punctuation mark in the manuscript.
- She is *fastidious* about her appearance, always ensuring her clothes are perfectly ironed.
- The chef's *fastidious* attention to detail resulted in a flawlessly presented and delicious meal.

EPHEMERAL

lasting for a very short time.

cherry blossoms falling. candle extinguishing. footprints erased by tide.

examples

- The beauty of the sunset was EPHEMERAL, fading within minutes.
- The artist created EPHEMERAL sand art that would be washed away by the tide.
- Fame in the digital age is often EPHEMERAL, lasting only until the next viral sensation.

TENUOUS

weak, thin, or fragile in strength or connection.

examples

- The TENUOUS rope stretched between the two cliffs swayed in the wind, shaking at any moment.
- His grasp on the job was TENUOUS; if sales didn't improve, he could lose his position.
- Her TENUOUS grasp on reality made it difficult for her to endure day to day life.

DOGMATIC

asserting opinions in an overly certain and unquestioning way.

chained against inquiry. resistant to change. ignoring irregular realities.

examples

- The politician's *dogmatic* refusal to consider opposing views alienated many voters.
- Despite the overwhelming scientific evidence, he remained *dogmatic* in his belief.
- Her *dogmatic* approach to the discussion left no room for compromise.

MUNDANE

ordinary, dull, or lacking excitement.

examples

- Despite the exciting news, his response was disappointingly MUNDANE and lacked any real enthusiasm.
- The daily commute to the office quickly became a MUNDANE part of her everyday life.
- The professor's lecture was a MUNDANE recitation of facts that failed to capture the students' interest.

to support or strengthen; to prop up.

strengthening what is weak

supporting what is at risk

reinforcing what needs stability

examples

- The new funding will **bolster** the organization's efforts to help more people.
- She spoke up to **bolster** her friend's confidence before the big presentation.
- A strong immune system can **bolster** your body against illness.

AMELIORATE

to improve or make something better.

make old locations safe & functional

construct safe, long lasting public spaces

which also secures a sustainable future

examples

- The new government's policies were designed to **AMELIORATE** the quality of life for all citizens.
- Donating food and supplies helped **AMELIORATE** the suffering of the flood victims.
- She volunteered at the community center to **AMELIORATE** the lives of many seniors.

BENEVOLENT

kind and generous toward others.

lifting others | offering shelter | guiding lost

examples

- Despite their own hardships, the BENEVOLENT couple donated a large sum to the local food bank.
- The queen was known for her BENEVOLENT rule, always prioritizing the well-being of her subjects.
- His BENEVOLENT nature led him to volunteer at the shelter every weekend, helping those in need.

CAPRICIOUS

given to sudden and unpredictable changes of mood or behavior.

weather vane spinning wildly in changing winds.

puppet with tangled strings moving unpredictably.

path constantly splitting into conflicting directions.

examples

- The ruler's **capricious** decisions left the court in constant disarray and uncertainty.
- He was known for his **capricious** nature, often changing his mind on important matters without warning.
- The weather in the mountains can be notoriously **capricious**, shifting from sunshine to snow in minutes.

RETICENT

reluctant to speak or reveal one's thoughts.

sealed lips withholding speech.

unopened letter concealing information.

candle glowing behind closed curtains.

examples

- The **reticent** witness refused to answer any questions during the trial.
- Despite knowing the answer, he remained **reticent** during the meeting.
- She was **reticent** about her past, sharing very few details with her friends.

MUNIFICENT

extremely generous or lavish in giving.

cornucopia overflowing with provisions.

hands offering coins freely to others.

fertile fields flourishing after generous rainfall.

examples

- The **munificent** donor funded the entire construction of the new community library.
- The queen was known for her **munificent** gifts to charities and the poor.
- He made a **munificent** contribution to the university's scholarship fund.

SAGACIOUS

having keen mental discernment and good judgment.

chess master anticipating several future moves.

wise owl observing hidden movement below.

lantern illuminating the safest path through darkness.

examples

- Her **sagacious** decision to invest early led to significant long-term gains.
- The **sagacious** leader navigated the political crisis with calmness and foresight.
- He offered **sagacious** advice that helped resolve the complex dispute.

PELLUCID

transparently clear; easy to understand.

still water revealing stones below.

sunlight passing clearly through glass.

map with a direct uncomplicated route.

examples

- His explanation made the complex subject **pellucid**.
- The report offered a **pellucid** view of the company's finances.
- She wrote in a **pellucid** style that everyone could understand.

PRODIGAL

wastefully extravagant or reckless with resources

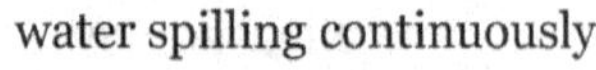

water spilling continuously

money vanishing into smoke

orchard stripped through excess

examples

- The prodigal son returned home after squandering his inheritance on wild living.
- Her prodigal spending on luxury goods left her with significant debt.
- The company's prodigal use of natural resources led to environmental criticism.

PERFUNCTORY

carried out with minimal effort or interest.

painter applying careless unfinished brushstrokes.

wilted garden receiving only a few drops of water.

student lazily skimming unread pages.

examples

- The doctor gave a perfunctory examination before declaring the patient well.
- Her perfunctory apology did little to mend the broken trust.
- A perfunctory glance at the report caused him to miss the crucial error.

INSIPID

lacking flavor, vigor, or interest.

colorless meal untouched.

identical buildings stretching endlessly.

wilted flower without fragrance.

examples

- The soup was insipid, tasting like warm water with absolutely no seasoning.
- The movie was a insipid romance, lacking chemistry between the leads and a compelling plot.
- Her insipid conversation about the weather quickly bored everyone at the dinner party.

MOLLIFY

to soothe or calm someone's anger or anxiety

waves slowly settling

hand calming frightened horse

blankets comforting travelers

examples

- The manager's gentle words helped to mollify the angry customer.
- Her attempt to mollify the situation only made him more upset.
- The company offered a full refund to mollify the dissatisfied client.

AUSTERE

severe or strict in manner, appearance, or attitude

plain wooden table

bare winter tree

ruler imposing order

examples

- The monastery was renowned for its austere way of life, free from any comfort or luxury.
- Her austere expression and severe tone made the students immediately silent and attentive.
- The designer's collection was noted for its austere simplicity and clean, straight lines.

EVANESCENT

soon passing out of sight, memory, or existence.

footprints disappearing beneath drifting snow

smoke dissolving into empty air

flower petals blowing away in strong wind

examples

- The rainbow's **evanescent** beauty faded quickly after the storm passed.
- Her fame proved to be **evanescent**, and she was soon forgotten.
- The scent of the flowers was **evanescent**, disappearing as quickly as it arrived.

REDOUBTABLE

formidable; inspiring fear or respect.

massive fortress overlooking smaller armies

thunderclouds advancing across a battlefield

lion calmly surveying frightened rivals

examples

- The **redoubtable** fortress proved impregnable to all attackers for centuries.
- His reputation as a **redoubtable** litigator caused many opponents to settle before trial.
- The team faced the **redoubtable** challenge of climbing the world's highest peak.

ASCETIC

practicing severe self-discipline and avoiding luxury.

plain bread beside untouched feasts

worn sandals beside ornate jewelry

single candle in empty chamber

examples

- The monk lived an ascetic life of solitude and prayer in the desert.
- Her ascetic diet and rigorous training prepared her for the marathon.
- He abandoned his wealthy lifestyle for the ascetic existence of a recluse.

PERNICIOUS

having a harmful effect, especially in a gradual or subtle way.

rot spreading slowly through healthy fruit.

dark smoke poisoning clear skies.

tiny roots cracking apart a stone wall over time.

examples

- The pernicious influence of propaganda slowly corrupted the minds of the people.
- A pernicious disease silently spread through the community before symptoms were noticed.
- Her pernicious lies had a gradual but devastating effect on their friendship.

SUPERCILIOUS

behaving as though one is superior to others.

dismissive gaze and chin | elevated towers above commoners | refusing common objects

examples

- The supercilious waiter made us feel unwelcome with his condescending attitude.
- Her supercilious manner at the meeting alienated her colleagues.
- He dismissed their concerns with a supercilious wave of his hand.

BELLICOSE

demonstrating aggression and willingness to fight

storm clouds colliding

crossed swords sparking

snarling wolf guarding

examples

- The bellicose leader's rhetoric incited the crowd to violence.
- Her bellicose behavior toward her neighbors led to numerous conflicts.
- The nation's bellicose stance alienated its allies.

BUCOLIC

relating to the pleasant aspects of the countryside and rural life.

peaceful cottage among grain fields | birds resting on rustic fence | winding country road

examples

- The artist painted a bucolic landscape of grazing sheep and rolling hills.
- They sought a bucolic retreat away from the noise and stress of the city.
- The novel beautifully described the bucolic charm of rural life in the valley.

CHIMERICAL

wildly fanciful or unrealistic

staircases leading upward into empty skies

fish swimming through clouds

castles balanced impossibly atop fragile towers

examples

- The architect's chimerical design for the floating city was dismissed as impossible.
- His chimerical dreams of perpetual motion machines led to financial ruin.
- The author created a chimerical world where rivers flowed backwards and trees grew upside down.

HAPHAZARD

lacking organization, planning, or order.

scattered puzzle pieces | tangled ropes | collapsing bookshelves

examples

- The haphazard arrangement of furniture made movement impossible.
- His haphazard approach to the project led to its failure.
- The garden grew in a haphazard manner, with weeds and flowers mixed.

FATUOUS

silly and pointless

ladder leading nowhere | bird perching on smoke | wheel spinning uselessly

examples

- His fatuous arguments about the weather were quickly dismissed by the scientists.
- She rolled her eyes at the fatuous comments made during the meeting.
- The fatuous proposal to build a bridge to nowhere was met with ridicule.

COGENT

clear, logical, and convincing.

puzzle pieces fitting together flawlessly

a straight beam of light cutting through darkness

a bridge supported by perfectly aligned arches

examples

- Her cogent argument convinced the jury of his innocence.
- The professor provided a cogent explanation of the complex theory.
- We need a cogent plan to address the company's financial challenges.

JOCULAR

fond of joking; humorous in a playful way.

joyful bells ringing in wind

laughing masks on stage

birds playfully chasing

examples

- His jocular comments during the meeting lightened the mood considerably.
- The friends shared jocular anecdotes about their recent trip, making everyone laugh.
- Despite the serious topic, her jocular approach kept the audience engaged and entertained.

GUILELESS

free from deceit or cunning; innocent and sincere

transparent water without hidden depths

unlocked gate welcoming travelers freely

child offering flowers sincerely to strangers

examples

- Her guileless nature made it impossible for her to suspect the treachery of others.
- The villagers' guileless hospitality was refreshing after the deceit of the city.
- A guileless answer can sometimes disarm even the most cynical questioner.

REVIEW QUIZ - PART 1

1. Which word means "deep, meaningful, or intellectually significant"?

A) Deceptive B) Profound C) Transient D) Meticulous

2. Which word means "misleading or giving a false impression"?

A) Authentic B) Eloquent C) Deceptive D) Flexible

3. What word describes something that is "genuine, real, and not false or copied"?

A) Authentic B) Volatile C) Fragmented D) Spontaneous

4. If something is "unstable and likely to change suddenly," it is:

A) Inevitable B) Persistent C) Dogmatic D) Volatile

5. Which word means "certain to happen or unavoidable"?

A) Conflicting B) Vague C) Inevitable D) Articulate

6. Someone who is "fluent, persuasive, and expressive in speech or writing" is:

A) Eloquent B) Obscure C) Indifferent D) Pragmatic

7. Which word describes ideas that are "incompatible or opposing one another"?

A) Coherent B) Intuitive C) Conflicting D) Subjective

8. Something that is "broken into disconnected parts" is:

A) Fragmented B) Superficial C) Discerning D) Reticent

9. To "make something seem less important or smaller" is to:

A) Distort B) Minimize C) Mitigate D) Augment

10. Which word means "to twist or misrepresent something"?

A) Reconcile B) Detract C) Ascertain D) Distort

11. Someone "showing little interest, concern, or emotion" is:

A) Capricious B) Indifferent C) Equivocal D) Dogged

12. If you are "continuing firmly despite difficulty," you are:

A) Persistent B) Ephemeral C) Tenuous D) Pensive

13. Which word means "temporary or lasting only a short time"?

A) Transient B) Ubiquitous C) Mundane D) Affluent

14. Being "willing or able to adapt to change" describes someone who is:

A) Dogmatic B) Flexible C) Reticent D) Spontaneous

15. Someone who is "holding opinions stubbornly as unquestionably true" is:

A) Meticulous B) Dogmatic C) Empathetic D) Articulate

16. Which word means "happening naturally without planning"?

A) Inevitable B) Spontaneous C) Persistent D) Coherent

17. A person who is "extremely careful and precise" is:

A) Meticulous B) Vague C) Superficial D) Pragmatic

18. Something "unclear or lacking specific details" is:

A) Eloquent B) Lucid C) Vague D) Articulate

19. Which word means "hidden, unclear, or difficult to understand"?

A) Authentic B) Obscure C) Profound D) Intrinsic

20. Someone "able to express ideas clearly and effectively" is:

A) Dogmatic B) Indifferent C) Articulate D) Fragmented

ANSWER KEY - PART 1

1. B (Profound)
2. C (Deceptive)
3. A (Authentic)
4. D (Volatile)
5. C (Inevitable)
6. A (Eloquent)
7. C (Conflicting)
8. A (Fragmented)
9. B (Minimize)
10. D (Distort)
11. B (Indifferent)
12. A (Persistent)
13. A (Transient)
14. B (Flexible)
15. B (Dogmatic)
16. B (Spontaneous)
17. A (Meticulous)
18. C (Vague)
19. B (Obscure)
20. C (Articulate)

REVIEW QUIZ - PART 2

2. To "create logical-sounding excuses for behavior" is to:

A) Rationalize B) Imply C) Mitigate D) Paradox

3. What word means "the ability to understand another person's feelings"?

A) Integrity B) Empathy C) Alienation D) Nuance

4. Someone who is "having mixed or conflicting feelings" is:

A) Intuitive B) Ambivalent C) Pragmatic D) Conventional

5. Which word means "different from traditional or commonly accepted ways"?

A) Unconventional B) Implicit C) Coherent D) Superficial

6. Something that is "following traditional or widely accepted ways" is:

A) Subjective B) Ambivalent C) Conventional D) Unconventional

7. "A feeling of isolation or separation from others" is called:

A) Empathy B) Correlation C) Alienation D) Constraint

8. Which word means "honesty and strong moral principles" or "wholeness"?

A) Paradox B) Integrity C) Nuance D) Causation

9. A "limitation or restriction" is a:

A) Constraint B) Correlation C) Causation D) Nuance

10. To "suggest something indirectly" is to:

A) Mitigate B) Imply C) Rationalize D) Coherent

11. If something is "based on personal opinions, feelings, or perspectives," it is:

A) Subjective B) Intuitive C) Pragmatic D) Implicit

12. Which word means "the act of causing something to happen"?

A) Causation B) Correlation C) Paradox D) Empathy

13. A "relationship or connection between two things" is a:

A) Paradox B) Nuance C) Correlation D) Causation

14. "A seemingly contradictory statement that may contain truth" is a:

A) Paradox B) Constraint C) Nuance D) Rationalize

15. Something "understood instinctively without conscious reasoning" is:

A) Subjective B) Implicit C) Intuitive D) Superficial

16. Which word means "concerned only with surface appearance" or "shallow"?

A) Unconventional B) Ambivalent C) Superficial D) Pragmatic

17. To "reduce the severity of something" is to:

A) Imply B) Rationalize C) Mitigate D) Constraint

18. Something that is "logical, consistent, and clearly connected" is:

A) Implicit B) Coherent C) Conventional D) Intuitive

19. If something is "suggested or understood without being directly stated," it is:

A) Implicit B) Explicit C) Superficial D) Pragmatic

20. A "subtle difference or distinction" is a:

A) Paradox B) Nuance C) Correlation D) Constraint

21. Someone who is "practical" and "focused on realistic results rather than ideals" is:

A) Pragmatic B) Subjective C) Ambivalent D) Intuitive

ANSWER KEY - PART 2

21. A (Rationalize)
22. B (Empathy)
23. B (Ambivalent)
24. A (Unconventional)
25. C (Conventional)
26. C (Alienation)
27. B (Integrity)
28. A (Constraint)
29. B (Imply)
30. A (Subjective)
31. A (Causation)
32. C (Correlation)
33. A (Paradox)
34. C (Intuitive)
35. C (Superficial)
36. C (Mitigate)
37. B (Coherent)
38. A (Implicit)
39. B (Nuance)

40. A (Pragmatic)

REVIEW QUIZ - PART 3

3. Which word means "lacking foresight or broad perspective; narrow-minded"?

A) Discerning B) Erudite C) Myopic D) Contentious

4. A "deviation from what is normal, expected, or typical" is an:

A) Equivocal B) Ostentatious C) Anachronism D) Aberration

5. To "increase, enlarge, or add to something" is to:

A) Reconcile B) Augment C) Ameliorate D) Bolster

6. Someone who is "able to make decisions quickly and confidently" is:

A) Reticent B) Capricious C) Tenacious D) Decisive

7. Which word means "showing steady and careful effort in work or duties"?

A) Lethargic B) Mundane C) Diligent D) Credulous

8. If something is "unclear or open to more than one interpretation," it is:

A) Lucid B) Ambiguous C) Fastidious D) Spurious

9. A person "having deep and extensive knowledge" is:

A) Erudite B) Indigent C) Benevolent D) Pensive

10. Something that is "clear, easy to understand, and mentally sharp" is:

A) Tenuous B) Clandestine C) Lucid D) Disparate

11. "Something placed outside its proper historical time period" is an:

A) Aberration B) Insular C) Cacophony D) Anachronism

12. Which word means "showing good judgment and insight"?

A) Credulous B) Discerning C) Altruistic D) Obstinate

13. Someone who is "extremely honest, careful, and attentive to detail" is:

A) Malleable B) Austere C) Scrupulous D) Dogged

14. If someone is "reserved; reluctant to speak openly," they are:

A) Reticent B) Affluent C) Magnanimous D) Ubiquitous

15. Something "designed to attract notice through excessive display" is:

A) Pristine B) Conventional C) Mundane D) Ostentatious

16. Someone who is "persistent and determined; unwilling to give up" is:

A) Tenuous B) Vacillate C) Tenacious D) Deference

17. To "replace something older or outdated" is to:

A) Ascertain B) Supersede C) Detract D) Lament

18. Which word means "changing suddenly and unpredictably"?

A) Dogmatic B) Fastidious C) Reverent D) Capricious

19. Something that is "severely simple; strict or plain in appearance" is:

A) Affluent B) Austere C) Ostentatious D) Ephemeral

20. If a statement is "open to multiple interpretations; uncertain in meaning," it is:

A) Vindicate B) Decisive C) Equivocal D) Discerning

21. Which word describes something "ordinary, dull, or lacking excitement"?

A) Mundane B) Profound C) Spontaneous D) Clandestine

22. To "restore harmony or bring into agreement" is to:

A) Detract B) Ameliorate C) Bolster D) Reconcile

41. Someone who is "isolated; narrow-minded from lack of contact with others" is:

A) Altruistic B) Benevolent C) Insular D) Erudite

22. Something "causing or likely to cause disagreement or argument" is:

A) Tenuous B) Contentious C) Disparate D) Malleable

23. A person "too ready to believe things without sufficient evidence" is:

A) Credulous B) Scrupulous C) Diligent D) Reticent

24. Being "kind and generous toward others" means you are:

A) Indigent B) Obstinate C) Benevolent D) Myopic

25. A connection that is "weak, thin, or fragile in strength or connection" is:

A) Tenacious B) Pristine C) Lethargic D) Tenuous

ANSWER KEY - PART 3

1. C (Myopic)
2. D (Aberration)

3. B (Augment)
4. D (Decisive)
5. C (Diligent)
6. B (Ambiguous)
7. A (Erudite)
8. C (Lucid)
9. D (Anachronism)
10. B (Discerning)
11. C (Scrupulous)
12. A (Reticent)
13. D (Ostentatious)
14. C (Tenacious)
15. B (Supersede)
16. D (Capricious)
17. B (Austere)
18. C (Equivocal)
19. A (Mundane)
20. D (Reconcile)
21. C (Insular)
22. B (Contentious)
23. A (Credulous)
24. C (Benevolent)
25. D (Tenuous)

REVIEW QUIZ - PART 4

4. Which word means "deeply thoughtful, often with a hint of sadness"?

A) Dogged B) Pensive C) Capricious D) Ostentatious

5. Someone who is "wealthy; having an abundance of money or resources" is:

A) Indigent B) Altruistic C) Austere D) Affluent

6. "Respectful submission to another's judgment or authority" is called:

A) Alienation B) Aberration C) Deference D) Anachronism

7. To "reduce the value or importance of something" is to:

A) Detract B) Augment C) Supersede D) Vindicate

8. Something "in perfect original condition; pure and unspoiled" is:

A) Spurious B) Pristine C) Disparate D) Equivocal

9. To "mourn or express deep sorrow" is to:

A) Reconcile B) Ascertain C) Vacillate D) Lament

10. "A harsh mixture of loud and unpleasant sounds" is a:

A) Nuance B) Constraint C) Cacophony D) Paradox

11. Someone who is "generous and forgiving, especially toward a rival or less powerful person" is:

A) Magnanimous B) Contentious C) Credulous D) Insular

12. A person "stubbornly refusing to change one's opinion or actions" is:

A) Malleable B) Obstinate C) Flexible D) Decisive

13. Which word means "sluggish; lacking energy or enthusiasm"?

A) Diligent B) Tenacious C) Discerning D) Lethargic

14. To "improve or make something better" is to:

A) Distort B) Detract C) Ameliorate D) Minimize

15. Something "kept secret or done secretly" is:

A) Ubiquitous B) Clandestine C) Obscure D) Lucid

16. A claim that is "false or misleading though appearing genuine" is:

A) Spurious B) Authentic C) Pristine D) Scrupulous

17. To "waver between choices or opinions" is to:

A) Ascertain B) Lament C) Vacillate D) Reconcile

18. Someone "showing selfless concern for the well-being of others" is:

A) Indigent B) Myopic C) Contentious D) Altruistic

19. Which word means "extremely attentive to detail; difficult to please"?

A) Lethargic B) Fastidious C) Tenuous D) Pensive

20. To "clear from blame or prove correct" is to:

A) Vindicate B) Augment C) Mitigate D) Rationalize

21. Elements that are "fundamentally different or distinct" are:

A) Coherent B) Implicit C) Disparate D) Spontaneous

22. Which word means "showing deep respect or admiration"?

A) Reticent B) Indifferent C) Ambivalent D) Reverent

23. Someone who is "poor or lacking basic necessities" is:

A) Affluent B) Indigent C) Magnanimous D) Ostentatious

42. A person who is "stubbornly persistent and determined" is:

A) Dogged B) Capricious C) Credulous D) Equivocal

23. Something that is "easily shaped, influenced, or changed" is:

A) Obstinate B) Dogged C) Malleable D) Austere

24. Which word means "present or appearing everywhere"?

A) Ephemeral B) Insular C) Clandestine D) Ubiquitous

25. To "discover or determine with certainty" is to:

A) Vacillate B) Ascertain C) Lament D) Detract

26. Something "lasting for a very short time" is:

A) Ephemeral B) Persistent C) Inevitable D) Ubiquitous

26. To "support, strengthen, or reinforce" is to:

A) Supersede B) Ameliorate C) Bolster D) Mitigate

ANSWER KEY - PART 4

1. B (Pensive)
2. D (Affluent)
3. C (Deference)
4. A (Detract)
5. B (Pristine)
6. D (Lament)
7. C (Cacophony)
8. A (Magnanimous)
9. B (Obstinate)
10. D (Lethargic)
11. C (Ameliorate)
12. B (Clandestine)
13. A (Spurious)
14. C (Vacillate)
15. D (Altruistic)
16. B (Fastidious)
17. A (Vindicate)
18. C (Disparate)
19. D (Reverent)
20. B (Indigent)
21. A (Dogged)
22. C (Malleable)
23. D (Ubiquitous)
24. B (Ascertain)
25. A (Ephemeral)
26. C (Bolster)

www.ingramcontent.com/pod-product-compliance
Lightning Source LLC
LaVergne TN
LVHW081253100826
845148LV00009B/1211

* 9 7 9 8 8 9 5 4 9 7 3 7 1 *